Thomas Hardy's Country

painted by Walter Tyndale RI

A WESSEX HOMESTEAD

SALMON

Published by
J Salmon Limited
100 London Road, Sevenoaks,
Kent TN13 1BB

First edition 1995
Second edition 1999
Third edition 2002

Designed by the Salmon Studio

Copyright © 1995 J Salmon Limited

ISBN 1 898435 25 1

Printed in England by
J Salmon Limited, Tubs Hill Works
Sevenoaks, Kent

THE GATEWAY, CERNE ABBAS
The 'Abbots Cernal' of the Wessex Novels

Coloured Illustrations

A WESSEX COTTAGE

AROUND DORCHESTER

Set almost in the heart of Dorset itself and surrounded by fertile meadows to the east, north and west and by gradually rising uplands which slope to the coast on its southern side, Dorchester is both picturesquely and well situated. It is a town with a long history, dating back to pre-Roman times, although, due to two devastating fires in the 17th century, little remains of old Dorchester. Of interest is undoubtedly St Peter's Church which stands on the north side of High West Street with the County Museum on one side and the Town Hall on the other. Outside stands the statue to the Rev. William Barnes, the 'Dorset poet', author of *Rural Poems in the Dorset Dialect* and opposite stands the building known as Judge Jeffrey's Lodging where the infamous judge stayed whilst presiding over the Bloody Assizes of 1685. The Napper's Mite in South Street was a charitable foundation in 1651 for the purpose of lodging ten poor men. Dorchester also boasts some outstanding archaeological remains. Close by are Maumbury Rings and two miles to the south lies Mai-Dun, 'the hill of strength', now known as Maiden Castle.

It is, however, as the centre of Thomas Hardy's Country that Dorchester is most celebrated. Hardy was born in 1840 in nearby Lower Bockhampton, in later life he lived at Max Gate and his heart was laid to rest in the churchyard at Stinsford. He borrowed the name of Wessex for the land in which his characters and stories are set, creating a world based on the places and countryside of his native Dorset. Thus Dorchester became 'Casterbridge' and the villages and landscape around the town feature particularly prominently in his works. Little Fordington, with its ancient church, appears in *The Mayor of Casterbridge* and Stinsford is 'Mellstock' in *Under the Greenwood Tree*. To the north is Cerne Abbas, with its chalk giant; this village is 'Abbot's Cernal' in *Far from the Madding Crowd* and other novels.

BOCKHAMPTON BANK NEAR DORCHESTER
The 'Mellstock Lane'
in *Under the Greenwood Tree*

FORDINGTON, DORCHESTER
The 'Back of Mixen Lane'
in *The Mayor of Casterbridge*

NEAR MAIDEN CASTLE, DORCHESTER
A scene in *The Mayor of Casterbridge*

THE RIVER FROME ABOVE DORCHESTER

SUMMER IN WESSEX

WAREHAM

The pleasant town of Wareham is situated on a ridge dividing the River Frome to the south and the Trent to the north. On passing through it the traveller in Wessex can scarcely realise that the town at one time occupied a position of importance but little now remains to show that as late as the 15th century Wareham was actually a seaport. The recession of the sea to its present day confines at Poole Harbour has robbed the town of its busy quays and ancient maritime characteristics.

In Saxon times Wareham must have been a town of some importance for we know that it was continually attacked and occupied by Danish pirates. Several kings of Wessex were buried in Wareham and it was also here, in the Church of St Mary, that the body of hapless Edward the Martyr, treacherously slain at Corfe Castle, is said to have been interred. St Martin's Church, perched upon a terrace at the northern end of the town, was founded by St Aldhelm in AD 698 on the site of a Roman temple. The town's street pattern almost certainly also dates from Saxon times although much of the architecture dates from the 18th century as a result of a disastrous fire in 1762.

In Thomas Hardy's Wessex novels Wareham is the 'Anglebury' of *The Return of the Native* and *The Hand of Ethelberta* and in places nearby he set some of the finest scenes in the greatest of his works *Tess of the D'Urbervilles*. Some five miles to the west is the little village of Wool, which Hardy named 'Wellbridge'. Here at the manor house, set amid pasture land and with the waters of the River Frome almost lapping against its walls, Tess and Angel Clare spend their ill-fated and all too brief honeymoon. It is here too that the powerful scene is enacted when Angel Clare carries Tess across the fields at the dead of night and places her in the ancient stone coffin of one of Bindon's abbots in the grounds of the old Cistercian abbey beyond the river.

THE VILLAGE OF WOOL
The 'Wellbridge' of *Tess of the D'Urbevilles*

WAREHAM
The 'Anglebury' of the Wessex Novels

THE SAXON CHURCH AT WAREHAM

BINDON ABBEY MILL
Where Angel Clare proposed to learn milling
in *Tess of the D'Urbevilles*

A WESSEX VILLAGE

THE HEART OF WESSEX

Both Thomas Hardy's grandfather and great-grandfather came from Puddletown which lies to the north-east of Dorchester. It is no surprise therefore that many of the most famous scenes in his novels take place in the villages and hamlets which lie in this neighbourhood, the very Heart of Wessex. Puddletown itself is a pretty little place with a fine church, where Troy spends the night in *Far from the Madding Crowd;* in the book Hardy named the village 'Weatherbury'. Close by is Lower Waterston where Waterston House, an imposing Jacobean manor, is the farmhouse of Bathsheba Everdene in the same novel.

The landscape hereabouts is typical of rural Dorset with sleepy hamlets and thatched homesteads dotting the countryside. Picturesque Affpuddle is the 'East Egdon' where Yeobright and Eustacia are married in *Return of the Native.* At Tincleton is the cottage home of Caroline Aspent in *Life's Little Ironies.* Close by is pretty little Moreton, best known for its associations with Lawrence of Arabia. He lived some three miles away at Clouds Hill and is buried in Moreton's 18th century parish church. Moreton is also supposed to be the location of 'Talbothays', the farm where Tess of the d'Urbervilles enters the service of the dairyman Crick.

To the east of Puddletown lies Bere Regis, 'Kingsbeare' in *Tess of the D'Urbervilles* and *Far from the Madding Crowd.,* and the setting for Woodbury Fair which played such an important part in the life of Sergeant Troy and Bathsheba in the latter novel. In olden times there were many such fairs held in the various towns of Wessex and Woodbury Hill, on the summit of which the fair took place, is an outstanding landmark for miles around, towering above the level of the quaintly placed Bere church, where the tombs of the Turbervilles can still be seen. Close by is Bere Heath, model for Hardy's Egdon Heath, "the vast tract of unenclosed wild".

WATERSTON HOUSE, LOWER WATERSTON

The Farmhouse of Bathsheba Everdene
in *Far from the Madding Crowd*

COTTAGE AT TINCLETON
The Home of Caroline Aspent of 'Fiddler of the Reels'
in *Life's Little Ironies*

THE MILL AND CHURCH AT AFFPUDDLE
The 'East Egdon Church' where Yeobright
and Eustacia were married in *Return of the Native*

COTTAGES AT MORETON
The Village near Talbothays
in *Tess of the D'Urbevilles*

THE RIVER FROME FROM BOCKHAMPTON BRIDGE
View from 'Lower Mellstock Bridge' of
"Fiddler of the Reels" in *Life's Little Ironies*

PUDDLETOWN
The 'Weatherbury' in *Far from the Madding Crowd*

IN PUDDLETOWN CHURCH

THE CHURCH AT BERE REGIS

'Kingsbere Church' in *Tess of the D'Urbevilles*

BERE REGIS
The 'Kingsbere' of *Tess of the D'Urbevilles*

BERE HEATH with Gallows Hill
The 'Egdon Heath' of the Wessex Novels

A WESSEX HAVEN

AROUND WEYMOUTH

South-west from Dorchester over the ridge of chalk downs towards the sea lies Weymouth, in the curve of one of the finest bays on the south coast. Beautifully situated and lapped in summer by the sapphire sea, there is from its seafront a panorama of rugged coast and breezy uplands. Travellers by the winding road which decends over the downs to the pretty village of Upwey will see Weymouth and distant Portland to best advantage. Weymouth is Budmouth Regis in *Under the Greenwood Tree* and *The Trumpet Major.* In the latter novel, a fine romance set in the stirring times of the Napoleonic Wars, the little village of Sutton Poyntz, nestling amid the hills a short distance inland from Weymouth Bay, plays a prominent part.

To the south of Weymouth lies Portland, 'The Isle of Slingers', where Hardy set his story *The Well-Beloved.* At one time Portland was an island, and is indeed still known as such, although now it is connected with the coast by Chesil Beach, the unique pebble ridge which extends westwards to Burton Bradstock and West Bay.

A very different place from Weymouth is Bridport, reached by a hilly road through Abbotsbury, with its famous Swannery and historic Tithe Barn, scene of the sheep shearing in *Far from the Madding Crowd.* Bridport, setting for the story *Fellow Townsmen,* is a picturesque little town lying in a hollow of the hills some mile and three-quarters inland from the mouth of the River Brit. There is a handsome brick Town Hall and a fine church, largely Perpendicular in style. The truer Bridport, the quaint little 'Port Bredy' of the Wessex novels, is the small seaside resort of West Bay with its busy harbour. The beach is of finest shingle and the narrow entrance to the quays is flanked on either side by cliffs of considerable height; as Hardy describes it "a gap in the rampart of hills which shut out the sea".

THE MILL COTTAGES AT SUTTON POYNTZ
The 'Overcombe' of *The Trumpet Major*

PORTLAND FROM THE NORTHERN SHORE OF WEYMOUTH BAY
The 'Isle of Slingers' of the Wessex Novels

THE TITHE BARN, ABBOTSBURY

The Scene of the sheep-shearing
in *Far from the Madding Crowd*

THE BRIDPORT ARMS
Bridport, the 'Port Bredy' of the Wessex Novels

THE PURBECK HILLS

CORFE CASTLE AND THE PURBECKS

Some five miles south-east of Wareham lies Corfe Castle, a small collection of grey-stoned houses dominated by the majestic ruins of the medieval castle. To the right of the mound on which the castle stands is Creech Barrow, towering above the other heights. From the summit of this hill there is a panoramic view of beauty and extent almost unequalled in Wessex. Below lies a wide stretch of moor extending towards Studland, in spring and summer ablaze with golden gorse and in autumn purple and ruddy with heather and bracken; in the middle distance are the silvery reaches of Poole Harbour. Close at hand stands the wonderful ruined pile of Corfe Castle, its original name, Corve's Gate, referring to the cleft in the line of the chalk hills which the castle was built to guard. The walls are redolent with the memory of the brutal murder of Edward the Martyr in AD 978, " the foulest deed which was ever committed" as the Anglo-Saxon Chronicle records. Centuries later a second act of treachery resulted in the betrayal of the castle to the Parliamentarians during the Civil War. Following this the castle was 'slighted' which resulted in its present-day ruinous appearance.

Around Corfe lies the beautiful Isle of Purbeck and along its southern shore, amidst wild and glorious coastal scenery, stand the seaside resort of Swanage and picturesque Lulworth Cove. Swanage fronts a sweeping bay, with an old town of shingle-roofed stone houses and a newer town which skirts the fine sandy beach. To the west is Lulworth Cove, a spot of singular beauty and charm with the old castle standing some mile or so inland from the exquisite little cove, circular in shape. Hereabouts the coast is spectacular with many dramatic rock formations. At Lulworth, thinly disguised as Lullstead, Hardy placed several of the scenes in his first novel *Desperate Remedies.*

THE KEEP, CORFE CASTLE
The 'Corvesgate Castle' of *The Hand of Ethelberta*

CORFE CASTLE FROM WEST STREET

A scene in *The Hand of Ethelberta*

STUDLAND HEATH
with Poole Harbour in the distance

LULWORTH COVE
The 'Lullstead Cove' in *Far from the Madding Crowd,*
Life's Little Ironies etc.

THE RIVER STOUR

WIMBORNE MINSTER AND POOLE

Wimborne Minster is situated in the picturesque and wooded valley through which flow the two rivers, the Stour and the Allen, or Win. Wimborne's recorded history dates back to earliest times; in 520 AD the Saxons and Britons did battle at Badbury Rings, an ancient earthwork still visible some three and a half miles to the north-west of the town. Wimborne takes its name from the splendid minster church built on the site of an 8th century monastery founded by St Cuthberga. The oldest parts of the minster date from the Norman period and the twin west towers and massive central tower make a fine spectacle particularly when viewed from afar across the watermeadows of the River Stour. A unique feature of the interior is the medieval orrery, an astronomical clock which shows the phases of the moon, the revolutions of the planets and the position of the sun.

To the south-west Wimborne is separated from Poole by a few miles or so of country lanes and open heathland. The traveller approaching Poole from this direction is rewarded with a prospect of great charm, embracing the beautiful harbour stretched out below and the lofty Purbeck Hills, which seem to shut the harbour in to the south. Eastward are the low hills of Parkstone and the bustling quays of Poole town itself. Poole, is one of the most ancient ports of the south of England and the quay is still busy with seagoing craft of every description. Behind a network of alleys run in and out of the larger and more solidly built red-brick houses which flank the quay. Amongst these are many picturesque bits of architecture including the stout Custom House and fine Guildhall with its sweeping staircases.

Poole Harbour itself is the second largest natural harbour in the world and a particular attraction is Brownsea Island, lying near the harbour mouth, with its castle, built on the orders of Henry VIII in 1548.

CANFORD HEATH NEAR POOLE

WIMBORNE MINSTER TOWERS
from the River Stour

A WESSEX DAIRY FARM

AROUND NORTH DORSET

Sherborne is pleasantly placed on the southern slope of a steep hill overhanging the valley of the River Yeo. The town's principal glory is the magnificent Abbey Church whose foundation dates back to the 8th century AD. The interior is of great beauty; both the nave and the choir are very fine and especially notable is the framed roof of the south transept. In the town itself, among the chief buildings of interest are the Abbey Conduit, built in 1349, standing at the bottom of Cheap Street and the Almshouses erected in 1448. In Hardy's novels Sherborne is 'Sherton Abbas' and features particularly in *The Woodlanders*.

The road from Sherborne to Shaftesbury passes through sixteen miles of some of the prettiest scenery in Wessex and crosses the famous Blackmore Vale. Known formerly as White Hart Forest, this fertile and secluded valley through which the little River Cale flows to meet the Stour is a spot well worthy of a visit from those who appreciate rural life. William Barnes, the Dorset poet, was a great admirer of the vale and he called it "the valley of sunny slopes, shady lanes, woody dales, picturesque trees and rivulets". It is through such scenery that the traveller approaches Shaftesbury, the 'Shaston' of *Jude the Obscure*. Truly a hill-top town Shaftesbury presents a wonderfully picturesque appearance, with its houses perched on the southern slope. Of the once beautiful abbey little now remains but the town is best known for Gold Hill, the steep cobbled street lined with thatched and tile-roofed cottages.

To the south lies Sturminster Newton where Hardy wrote *Return of the Native* and Blandford Forum, 'Shottsford' in the same novel and a perfect Georgian market town, rebuilt after a terrible fire in 1731.

LONG STREET AND ABBEY CONDUIT, SHERBORNE

The 'Sherton Abbas' of *The Wessex Novels*

BLACKMORE VALE FROM SHAFTESBURY
A scene in *Jude the Obscure*

INTERIOR OF SHERBORNE ABBEY